Fish

Elizabeth Nonweiler

raintree

cod

batfish

scat

shark

boxfish

lungfish

reef fish

garfish

frogfish

basslet

ribbonfish

parrotfish

Interesting facts about the pictures

page 2: **Cod** live in deep cold salty water in the Atlantic Ocean. They are often caught and cooked for fish and chips.

page 3: **Batfish** like to live in muddy places on the coast of warm parts of the ocean. This is a round batfish. It is very thin.

page 4: **Scats** are small fish that usually live in warm parts of the ocean. Some are kept by people in aquariums. They can live for 20 years.

page 5: **Sharks** live in the ocean. This is a great white shark. Some sharks can swim 80 kilometres in one day. They eat small fish and hardly ever hurt people.

page 6: **Boxfish** have heavy scales like plates on their bodies, so they move slowly. The adults look a bit like a box, but this young one is more round.

page 7: **Lungfish** can breathe air with their lungs. They live in fresh water, but if the water dries up, they can burrow in mud and stay alive until the rain comes again.

page 8: **Reef fish** live on coral reefs with hundreds of other sea creatures. They are colourful like the coral, so they are good at hiding from bigger fish that want to eat them.

page 9: **Garfish** lay their eggs in shallow water in spring and then move to the open sea. Some live in the sea around the British Isles. They have long jaws with sharp teeth.

page 10: **Frogfish** grow to about one metre long. They can eat other fish as big as themselves with their enormous jaws and stretchy stomachs. This is a baby frogfish.

page 11: **Basslet** are small fish that live in coral reefs and lagoons. This one is sometimes called a sea goldie. Basslet eat tiny sea animals called plankton.

page 12: A **ribbonfish** lives in very deep cold water. It has only one fin along the whole length of its back. Some ribbonfish are more than two metres long.

page 13: A **parrotfish** has a small mouth with little teeth that looks a bit like a parrot's beak. Its teeth gets worn down by eating plants and plankton, but they keep growing.

Letter-sound correspondences

Level 1 books cover the following letter-sound correspondences. Letter-sound correspondences highlighted in **green** can be found in this book.

ant	**b**ig	**c**at	**d**og	**e**gg	**f**ish	**g**et	**h**ot	**i**t
jet	**k**ey	**l**et	**m**an	**n**ut	**o**ff	**p**an	**qu**een	**r**un
sun	**t**ap	**u**p	**v**an	**w**et	bo**x**	**y**es	**z**oo	

du**ck**	fi**sh**	**ch**ips	si**ng**	**th**in **th**is	k**ee**p	l**oo**k m**oo**n	**ar**t	c**or**n